DATE DUE

GAYLORD

PRINTED IN U.S.A.

DEC   2004

CONFLICT: INDIA vs. PAKISTAN

DAVID DOWNING

Raintree

Chicago, Illinois

Library of Congress Cataloging in Publication Data
Downing, David, 1946-
  Conflict: India vs. Pakistan / David Downing.
      p. cm. -- (Troubled world)
Summary: Takes an in-depth look at the ongoing conflict and troubles
between the countries of India and Pakistan.
Includes bibliographical references and index.
  ISBN 1-4109-0181-5 (library binding-hardcover)
  1. India--Foreign relations--Pakistan--Juvenile literature. 2.
Pakistan--Foreign relations--Pakistan--Juvenile literature. [1.
India--Foreign relations--Pakistan. 2. Pakistan--Foreign
relations--India.] I. Title: India versus Pakistan. II. Title. III.
Series.
  DS450.P18D68 2003
  327.5405491'09045--dc21
                                    2003002171

Printed and bound in China by South China Printing Company.
08 07 06 05 04
10 9 8 7 6 5 4 3 2 1

Acknowledgments
The publishers would like to thank the following for permission to reproduce photographs:
Pp. 7, 10, 16, 17, 19, 21, 24, 27, 33, 36, 42 Topham Picturepoint; pp. 9, 13, 26, 28, 31, 34, 44,
46, 48, 51, 56, 58 Popperfoto; pp.12, 32 Corbis (Bettmann) pp. 15 39 Corbis; p.40 Corbis
(Zen Icknow); p. 50 Image Works/Topfoto; p. 52 Getty Images; p. 55 Corbis (Chris Collins
studio).

Cover photograph of BJP demonstrators near the Pakistani Embassy, New Delhi, India,
1990. Reproduced with permission of Topham/AP.

Contents

Words that appear in the text in bold, **like this**, are explained in the glossary.

India and Pakistan: A Troubled History

At the beginning of the 21st century, the Indian subcontinent—
that area of Asia bordered by the sea to the east, south, and
west, and hemmed in by the Himalaya mountain range to the
north—was home to three of the world's most populous countries:
India, Pakistan, and Bangladesh. According to military experts, the
subcontinent was also home to the most dangerous border in the
world, that between India and Pakistan. A nuclear war, they said,
was more likely to begin here than anywhere else on Earth.

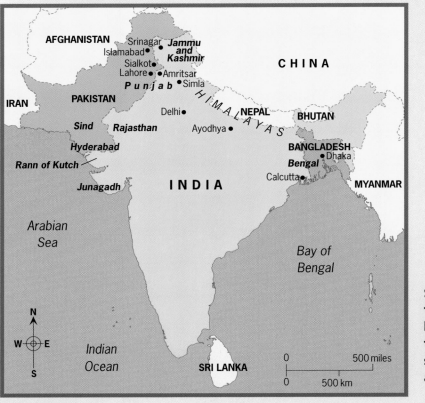

Some of these borders on the Indian subcontinent are disputed.

The hostility between India and Pakistan has a long history. Since
they were granted independence from British rule in 1947, the two
states have gone to war on three occasions (1947, 1965, and 1971),
and narrowly avoided war on several others.

The conflicts have been fierce, and sometimes hard to comprehend.
One part of the border in the disputed Kashmir region was never
marked out. The reason was simple: the land concerned, which lay
at over 15,978 feet (4,870 meters) above sea level and included two

huge glaciers, seemed of no use to anyone. But in 1984 the two countries began stationing their soldiers on the Siachen Glacier. Since then thousands have been killed, some by enemy fire, but many more by simple accidents. Why are the

Population (in millions):			
	1950	1975	2000
India	350	601	1014
Pakistan	40	75	142
Bangladesh	–	77	129

soldiers there? According to one Pakistani commando officer, "It's madness. Total madness. Siachen is hell on Earth. We're fighting the bloody Indians to prevent them from grabbing what we say is our rightful part of hell. That's how much we hate each other."

But why are relations between these two countries so bad? India is a predominantly **Hindu** state, Pakistan almost exclusively **Muslim.** But there are many examples of states following different religions who make good neighbors. The border between them has never been finally agreed upon, but it has been in place now for more than half a century.

So where does the discord come from? To understand this it is necessary to return to the reason these two states were born and the violent circumstances of their birth.

Three religions

In 2002 Hindus made up 81 percent of the Indian population and 2 percent of the Pakistani population. Hindus believe in a supreme spiritual force called Brahma, which finds expression through a multitude of gods, and the cycle of birth, death, and rebirth known as reincarnation. Hindu society is traditionally divided into rigid castes or classes, each of which is associated with a different job, such as shopkeeping or cleaning.

Muslims made up 97 percent of the Pakistani population, but only 12 percent of the Indian population. Muslims believe in one God, whose prophet was Muhammad, and whose teachings are written out in a holy book called the Koran.

Sikhs made up 2 percent of the Indian population (almost all of them in the northwestern region of the Punjab), and they also believe in one God. Like Hindus they believe in reincarnation, but unlike Hindus Sikhs reject castes, believing that people should live and work as equals.

5

Turning Point: Partition

When the British originally arrived in India during the early 1600s, the subcontinent was divided up into hundreds of states of different sizes. The British took direct control of the ones they considered most important, but allowed others some degree of self-rule. The India that the British ruled, directly or indirectly, from the mid-18th century to the mid-20th century, included present-day India, Pakistan, Bangladesh, Myanmar (formerly Burma), Sri Lanka (formerly Ceylon), and the Himalayan kingdoms of Nepal, Bhutan, and Sikkim. Myanmar and the Himalayan kingdoms were always considered separate pieces of British India, but the remainder was seen as a whole by both the British and the Indians, even though it included many **ethnic** groups (such as the Bengalis and Tamils) speaking different languages, and several religions, such as Hinduism, **Islam**, and Sikhism. During the early years of the Indian independence movement—from the late 1800s to the 1930s—it was assumed by almost everyone that the British would eventually grant independence to a single state, not three states.

The fight for independence was spearheaded by the All-India Congress Party. The "All-India" part was significant: the Congress claimed to represent all of India's ethnic and religious communities, and did indeed include representatives from them in its leadership. Its aim was a **secular** state in which all communities would have the freedom to worship as they chose. This was not just wishful thinking. Leaders like Mahatma Gandhi and Jawaharlal Nehru knew that India, like most other countries, had a long history of occasional hostility between its various communities. They had no illusions that independence would solve everything. This was why they believed that the state had to stand above religion and act as an impartial judge and instrument of healing whenever such disputes occurred.

The need for Pakistan

Most **Hindus** were convinced by this argument. They were after all the majority community, forming some 70 percent of the total population. There was no chance that their interests would be ignored in a new **democratic** India. But for many **Muslims**, who formed roughly 25 percent of the population, the prospect of living with a permanent Hindu majority was worrying. As independence grew nearer, a steady rise in the number of violent clashes between the two communities turned anxiety into fear. The only answer, many Muslims decided, was partition. Partition meant the division of British India into two states: one that included all the Muslim-majority areas, and one that included all the Hindu-majority areas.

The British did not like this idea, and neither did the All-India Congress Party. To the Congress Party, partition was a surrender to communal hostility, when the aim was to rise above it. But the Congress leaders were unable to persuade the Muslim leader, Muhammad Ali Jinnah, that an independent Muslim state was unnecessary. Soon after World War II ended, with independence looming, Jinnah's Muslim League began a campaign for an independent state to be called Pakistan.

Violent disturbances broke out across the area, and over the next eighteen months they increased, until the whole country seemed on the verge of **civil war.** The British, struggling with economic troubles at home and eager to leave India as soon as possible, gave in to the Muslim League's demands. The Congress party, impatient for power after so many decades, also bowed to what now seemed inevitable and accepted partition.

Muslims flee from India during the 1947 Partition on this overcrowded train leaving Delhi for West Pakistan.

Partition

When independence was granted in 1947, the states directly ruled by the British were given to either India or Pakistan, depending on whether their population was mostly **Hindu** or **Muslim.** Muslim regions lay on both the east and west side of India—these separate territories became East and West Pakistan, and were part of the same country. For most states the decision was reasonably clear cut, but both Punjab in the northwest and Bengal in the northeast had roughly equal populations of Hindus and Muslims. In the Punjab there was also a large **Sikh** minority that had no desire to live in the new Pakistan.

Flight

"They fled in their bullock carts or, if they never owned a cart or it was taken from them, they fled on foot, whole families, adults carrying children, carrying the sick in baskets, carrying the aged on their shoulders. Frequently the sick were abandoned and left to die on the dusty road ... vultures hovered the line of march waiting for weary wanderers to drop to the ground...."
American journalist Louis Fischer, describing the migrations that accompanied the 1947 partition

Bengal and the Punjab had to be hurriedly divided between the two new countries. People desperately scrambled for the safety of their own religious communities; religion had divided their land and panic had set in. The panic and fear turned to hysteria, and violence erupted on an almost unbelievable scale.

Fifty-five years later, it is hard to imagine the enormity of what took place in Bengal and, particularly, in the Punjab. During the last chaotic months of 1947, over half a million people were killed in communal violence—for no other reason than the fact that they belonged to a particular religious community. They did not die as soldiers in battle; they died as families and individuals, caught in the open or trapped on trains, bludgeoned, hacked, or beaten to death. It was as if two peoples had gone insane with fear and hatred, and the memories of this insanity, its horrors and hatred, would be handed down from generation to generation. Many Hindus and Muslims were left with the lasting belief that each community's deepest wish was the destruction of the other.

Exceptions to the rule

In those states that the British had ruled indirectly, the local ruler was supposed to follow the same principles of **accession** and join either India or Pakistan. In three cases this did not happen. In Junagadh, a Muslim ruler of a Hindu majority population tried to join Pakistan. In Hyderabad, a Muslim ruler with a Hindu majority population tried to declare independence. Both were surrounded by Indian territory, and were forced into joining India. In the state of Jammu and Kashmir, by contrast, a Hindu ruler with a Muslim majority population hesitated and then broke the rules by acceding to India. Pakistan objected. Since Jammu and Kashmir had borders with both India and Pakistan, both countries could send in forces and each prevent the other from gaining complete control. The resulting dispute has remained unresolved to this day.

Biography—Jawaharlal Nehru

Born in Allahabad to a prominent family, Nehru (1889–1964) studied law at Cambridge University in Britain before joining the independence-seeking All-India National Congress in 1918. Imprisoned nine times by the British, he later played a leading role in the negotiations that led to independence in 1947, and became India's first prime minister. In domestic affairs he promoted industrialization and sought to reinforce the **secular,** multicultural tradition with which the Congress had always been associated.

Nehru's conviction that Kashmir should be part of India led to a breach with his old friend Sheikh Abdullah, whom he feared was plotting for Kashmiri independence. As a result Nehru missed India's best chance of giving Kashmir a meaningful degree of self-government. Nehru died in 1964, and was eventually succeeded as Congress leader and prime minister by both his daughter, Indira Gandhi, and grandson, Rajiv Gandhi.

Prime minister of India Jawaharlal Nehru visits London in October 1949.

Kashmir

The region now known as Kashmir, which in the years before independence formed the state of Jammu and Kashmir, is a land of deep valleys and high mountains, roughly the size of Oregon. Its northern and western areas—Gilgit-Baltistan and Ladakh—have only a tiny population. Most Kashmiris live in the southern areas of Poonch and Jammu and, particularly, the Vale of Kashmir. The Vale, a beautiful oval bowl scraped out of the mountains, some 80 miles (130 kilometers) long and 25 miles (40 kilometers) wide, is the heart of Kashmir, home to its largest concentration of people and its capital city, Srinagar.

Kashmir's population—about 4 million in 1947, and about 10 million by the end of the 1990s—is a patchwork of religious identities. Ladakh is mostly **Buddhist,** Gilgit-Baltistan and Poonch almost exclusively **Muslim,** and Jammu overwhelmingly **Hindu.** The Vale, though mixed, has a large Muslim majority. Estimates indicate that Kashmir is 77 percent Muslim, 20 percent Hindu, 2 percent **Sikh,** and 1 percent Buddhist.

Kashmir is a land of snow-covered mountains, dark forests, and swift-flowing streams.

Accession

In August 1947 Kashmir had a Hindu ruler named Hari Singh. When the British granted independence to India and Pakistan, Singh was asked to choose between them. Singh refused to commit himself. The fact that the state had a Muslim majority suggested Pakistan, but there was no evidence to show that the majority of Kashmiris actually favored this course. Most Muslim Kashmiris supported the National Conference party (once the Muslim Conference), which was led by a Muslim, Sheikh Abdullah. Like many of his friends in the Congress, Sheikh Abdullah was more interested in land reform and social progress than religious solidarity. He believed that, on balance, opting for India rather than Pakistan offered a better chance of achieving his goals. India, he said later, had the "goal of a **secular democracy** based upon justice, freedom, and modern democracy," whereas Pakistan was "a **feudal** state" in which "a clique was trying to maintain itself in power."

The disputed region of Kashmir.

Through September and into October 1947, Hari Singh remained undecided. If he hoped that India and Pakistan would eventually give up and leave him and Kashmir alone, he was soon disillusioned. In mid-October **Muslims** in the Poonch region rose up in rebellion and, aided by the new authorities in Pakistan, began advancing down the Jhelum Valley toward the Vale and Srinagar. Panic-stricken, Hari Singh asked for Indian military help.

Indian Prime Minister Nehru agreed to send troops on two conditions: one, that Hari Singh sign the Instrument of **Accession** that would join Kashmir to India, and two, that Sheikh Abdullah offer his support. The accession itself involved two more conditions. First, Kashmir was to enjoy a special status within India: Although decisions concerning foreign affairs, defense, and communications would be made by the central government in New Delhi, all other decisions would be left to the Kashmiri Government in Srinagar. Second, a vote would be held at some unspecified date in which all Kashmiris would be able to make a final choice between India and Pakistan.

War
Hari Singh, fearful of the Muslims advancing up the valley, signed the letter of accession. Indian troops were airlifted into the Vale, and the rebels were prevented from reaching Srinagar. Over the next few weeks, the two sides grabbed what land they could.

Indian troops took firm possession of Jammu, Ladakh, and the Vale, while **Muslim irregulars** took control of Poonch and the Gilgit-Baltistan region. There was frequent fighting and many casualties, with atrocities committed by both sides. The worst of these was the attack on Baramula by Muslim irregulars, in which some 3,000 of the small town's 14,000 population were murdered.

India took the dispute to the **United Nations (UN)**. The **accession** of Kashmir to India was legal, the Indians argued, and Pakistan's support for those Muslims fighting against it was aggression. The accession was illegal, the Pakistanis countered, because Hari Singh had already been overthrown when he signed it. They demanded that the people of Kashmir be allowed to decide, and, in this at least, the UN agreed with Pakistan. It ordered both countries to withdraw their forces, and for a **plebiscite** (vote) to be held.

Neither side showed any inclination to withdraw its forces. The official Pakistani Army became more openly involved in May 1948, though with little apparent effect. Pakistan was at a military disadvantage. It had no hope of pushing the superior Indian forces out of **Hindu** Jammu or the mostly Muslim Vale. The Indians, though stronger, had little chance of driving the Pakistanis out of the difficult-to-reach mountainous areas they held in the mountainous west and north, areas that were now called "Azad (Free) Kashmir" by the Pakistanis. Realizing that they could not dislodge each other, the two sides agreed to a **cease-fire** on January 1, 1949.

Indian soldiers arrive in Srinagar to fight Pakistani troops for ownership of the Kashmir region of India, November 1947.

Biography—Sheikh Abdullah

Sheikh Abdullah (1905–1982) was born near the Kashmiri capital of Srinagar. In the 1930s he formed the All Jammu and Kashmir Muslim Conference (renamed the National Conference in 1938), which led the Muslim Kashmiri opposition to the local ruler (or maharajah) and his British backers. In 1947 he accepted the state's accession to India, partly because he thought that any bid for independence would be quashed, and partly because he believed that India was more likely than Pakistan to help the poor. He did make it clear that his acceptance was conditional on India allowing Kashmir a considerable degree of self-government, or **autonomy.**

Unfortunately for Sheikh Abdullah and for Kashmir, his occasional statements in favor of Kashmiri independence, and his continual demands for the autonomy that India had promised, persuaded Nehru and other Indian leaders that he might be secretly plotting a **secession.** As a consequence he was frequently arrested.

Released from prison in 1972, Sheikh Abdullah became Kashmir's prime minister in 1975, and signed the Kashmir Accord with Indira Gandhi's Congress Government in Delhi. The accord was essentially a watered-down version of the deal made between him and Congress in 1947, and some Muslim Kashmiris accused him of betraying his people's interests. The seven years that followed, however, were a period of relative calm and prosperity in Kashmir. In 1982 Sheikh Abdullah died a national hero.

Sheikh Abdullah's resistance to foreign rule of his country earned him the nickname "Lion of Kashmir."

India and the Vale

With the fighting over, attention switched to the all-important Vale. Would the Kashmiri Muslim majority who lived there accept Indian rule? For a while it seemed possible. Sheikh Abdullah's National Conference won the state elections in 1951, deprived Hari Singh of his powers, and began implementing its program of social and economic reforms. Kashmir's special position, which gave it a semi-independent status within India, was confirmed in the Delhi Accord of 1952.

The ink had hardly dried on the Delhi Accord when the situation began to deteriorate. The **Buddhist** monasteries of Ladakh and the **Hindu** landlords of Jammu were both upset by Sheikh Abdullah's land reforms, which threatened to take away much of their land. In New Delhi some Congress leaders decided that Sheikh Abdullah would never be content with only semi-independence, and in August 1953 he was arrested on charges of plotting to take Kashmir out of the union. He would spend most of the next 20 years in jail.

An administration more agreeable to New Delhi took over, and money for improving health, education, and transportation was poured into Kashmir. In return for this display of generosity, **Muslims** were expected to forget about Kashmir's "special status," and the promise of a **plebiscite.** Unsurprisingly, they did not. By ignoring the Kashmiri desire for a real measure of self-government within India, India's rulers had wasted their best chance of a lasting settlement.

According to the United Nations...

- "The Government of Pakistan should undertake to use its best endeavors ... to secure the withdrawal from the State of Jammu and Kashmir of tribesmen and Pakistani nationals not normally resident therein who have entered the State for the purposes of fighting...."

- "The Government of India should undertake that there will be established in Jammu and Kashmir a Plebiscite Administration to hold a plebiscite as soon as possible on the question of the accession of the State to India or Pakistan."

Two excerpts from UN Resolution 47, adopted by the Security Council on April 21, 1948. The first calls on Pakistan to remove its armed supporters from Kashmir; the second calls on India to then allow a vote of all Kashmiris to decide which country they wish to join.

During India's war with China in 1962, officials called on young women to form a second line of defense.

The failure of diplomacy

Kashmir remained a high-profile international problem, and a source of continuing friction between India and Pakistan. A stream of **UN resolutions** were passed and ignored in 1948–1949, and in both 1950 and 1951 the two countries teetered on the brink of another war. Both claimed they were willing to hold a plebiscite, but neither did anything to make one happen. Then, in 1954, Pakistan joined the South-East Asia Treaty Organization (SEATO), a military alliance that included both the United States and Britain. India felt threatened and withdrew its agreement to a plebiscite. A year or so later, Nehru offered a permanent partition of Kashmir along the **cease-fire** line. Pakistan refused.

In the autumn of 1962, India lost a brief and humiliating border war with China. In the aftermath Nehru asked the West for help. He was told he could have it only if he talked to Pakistan about Kashmir. The six rounds of talks that eventually took place ended in complete deadlock. This, of course, suited India better than Pakistan—India, after all, was reasonably satisfied with its share of Kashmir. The Pakistanis, by contrast, were getting desperate. UN resolutions and negotiations between the two sides had failed to shift the Indian position. Perhaps only force could unlock the gates to the Vale.

Turning Point: The War of 1965

By 1965 Pakistan felt it had run out of peaceful options for securing control of Kashmir. The Indians were prepared to talk, but not actually to offer anything. Pakistan's alliance with the United States had antagonized the Soviet Union, which now supported India's position at the **United Nations,** and promised to **veto** any UN move to question India's position in Kashmir. There seemed little chance that a **plebiscite** would ever be held to determine the wishes of the Kashmiri people. But Pakistan's leaders had to do something. With each year that passed, Kashmir was more tightly bound to India. Time was running out.

Pakistani soldiers pass a damaged Indian tank in the early stages of the 1965 war.

Was war a realistic option? Were Pakistan's chances of military victory any greater in 1965 than they had been in 1947? The military, which had now ruled Pakistan since 1958, believed that war could be their best chance. For one thing India's army had performed dismally in the 1962 border war with China, and there was no reason to think that it would perform any better against Pakistan. For another they expected more active support from the people of the Vale. In 1947 the Vale's **Muslims** had preferred Sheikh Abdullah to Pakistan, but the Sheikh was in prison again, and Indian rule was now less popular. In 1963 there had almost been an uprising when someone stole a sacred relic from a Srinagar mosque. Only the relic's return had brought widespread disturbances to an end.

If the military position for Pakistan really was more favorable than it had been in 1947, it might not remain so for long. The defeat by China had shocked the Indian Government, and great efforts were under way to improve the Indian armed forces. Pakistan's leaders believed that, with each year that passed, their chances of success grew slimmer.

In March 1965 one final piece of the puzzle fell into place. During a visit to China, Pakistan's President Ayub Khan and Foreign Minister Zulfiquar Ali Bhutto were given what they believed was a promise of Chinese help in any future war with India.

Chinese leader Mao Zedong welcomes Pakistan's President Ayub Khan to Beijing in March 1965.

Invaders or liberators?

"The period of the infiltration campaign was characterized by intense, hectic activity throughout the [Jammu and Kashmir] theater, with special emphasis in the Valley. The raiders and [our] own forces marched and counter-marched all over the inhospitable terrain in a vast game of hide and seek. Several times during the day, the opponents met, clashed, and reeled apart in a series of bloody actions, weaving a confused pattern hard to unravel."
Lieutenant General Harbaksh Singh, who commanded India's forces on the western front during the 1965 war, describes the initial confrontation with Pakistani infiltrators in Kashmir

The Rann of Kutch

Rather than leap straight into a full-scale war in Kashmir, the Pakistani leadership decided on a small rehearsal to test India's resolve. They chose the Rann of Kutch, a desolate area of salt marsh straddling the southern end of the border between India and West Pakistan. For much of the year, this region lay underwater; for the rest it was inhabited by wild donkeys and flamingos. Since few humans ever came there, the border had never been properly marked out, and was disputed by the two countries. It seemed an ideal spot for testing India's military strength and determination.

In January 1965 the Pakistani Army began behaving more aggressively, provoking incidents with Indian patrols and moving their own bases further forward. Over the next few months, these hostilities gradually escalated, until by April several hundred tanks were involved in a series of rolling battles, which only ended when the Indians retreated 25 miles (40 kilometers). The Pakistanis were overjoyed; the performance of the Indian military had been as poor in the Rann of Kutch as it had been against the Chinese. International pressure produced a **cease-fire** early in May, but the Pakistani military was already preparing for another campaign, this time in Kashmir.

Pakistan's case

*"If a **Muslim** majority can remain a part of India, then the raison d'être [reason to exist] of Pakistan collapses. These are the reasons why India, to continue her domination of Jammu and Kashmir, defies international opinion and violates her pledges. For the same reason, Pakistan must unremittingly continue her struggle for the right of self-determination of this subject people. Pakistan is incomplete without Jammu and Kashmir both territorially and ideologically. It would be fatal if, in sheer exhaustion or out of intimidation, Pakistan were to abandon the struggle, and a bad compromise would be tantamount to abandonment; which might, in turn, lead to the collapse of Pakistan."*
Zulfiquar Ali Bhutto, then Pakistan's foreign minister, explaining in 1969 why Pakistan could not afford to abandon its claim to Kashmir

Kashmir and the Punjab

Late in May 1965, the Pakistanis gathered a force of about 5,000 men in the town of Murree, close to the cease-fire line dividing Kashmir. In early August these men, dressed as local inhabitants and carrying only small arms, began slipping across the line into Indian-controlled territory. Their purpose was to start a rebellion against Indian rule in the Vale, but they soon ran into difficulties. The local people proved more inclined to watch and wait than to join in. Some even alerted the Indian authorities to the presence of the intruders.

Indian troops search for Muslim infiltrators in Kashmir during the 1965 war.

Undeterred, the Pakistani leadership moved to the next phase of its plan, sending its own uniformed troops across the border to support the hoped-for rebellion. The Indians retaliated by sending their troops across the cease-fire line to occupy a large area of "Azad Kashmir." The Pakistanis hit back even harder. On August 31 they launched Operation Grand Slam, an invasion of southern Kashmir, spearheaded by 70 tanks. The Indians brought in their air force for the first time, but this failed to halt the Pakistanis, who by September 5 were close to cutting the only major route connecting Kashmir with the rest of India.

Unable to meet this threat directly, the Indians launched two powerful attacks in the Punjab on September 6, one directed against the road and rail center Sialkot, the other against Pakistan's second city, Lahore. The initial success of these attacks, and the threat they posed to the heart of Pakistan, forced the withdrawal of those Pakistani units threatening Kashmir.

The Indian advance was stopped outside Lahore, and a few days later the largest tank battle of the war was fought outside Sialkot. This ended inconclusively, and the war as a whole was now approaching stalemate, as both sides ran low on ammunition. On September 21–22 the two governments bowed to international pressure for a **cease-fire.**

A promise broken

*"It is now too late to talk of a **plebiscite**.... Any plebiscite now would definitely amount to questioning the **integrity** of India. It would raise the issue of **secession**—an issue on which the U.S. once fought a **civil war**.... We cannot and will not tolerate a second partition of India on religious grounds."*
Indian Prime Minister Indira Gandhi, speaking to a U.S. audience in 1966. By using the United States's own history she hoped to gain sympathy for India's position on Kashmir.

Aftermath
Pakistan's second attempt to take the Vale away from India by force had ended in failure. The Indian Army had proven stronger and more determined than expected, and the Chinese had decided it was safer not to interfere on Pakistan's side. The **Muslim** Kashmiris had failed to welcome their intended liberators with open arms. The Pakistani leadership had made, not for the last time, the mistake of confusing anti-India sentiment with pro-Pakistan sentiment. In 1965 most Muslim Kashmiris probably favored a split with India, but that did not mean they wanted to join Pakistan.

Pakistan's President Ayub Khan (bottom right) signs the 1966 peace agreement in the Soviet city of Tashkent.

Peace talks were held at Tashkent in the Soviet Union, with Soviet Premier Alexei Kosygin acting as mediator. Given that the war had ended with Indian troops in possession of a significant portion of their territory, the Pakistanis had few cards to play. They accepted a return to the *status quo ante* (the situation before), and signed an agreement not to use force in future to settle the dispute between the two countries. The dispute, however, remained.

The Chinese ultimatum

Despite its promise of help to Pakistan, China's only contribution to the war was a two-part ultimatum to India, delivered only days before the cease-fire. The first half of the ultimatum demanded the dismantling of fortifications that the Chinese claimed the Indians had erected near their mutual border. The second part demanded the immediate return of 800 sheep and 60 yaks that the Chinese implied had been stolen by Indians. Both the Soviet Union and the United States swiftly warned the Chinese against interfering, and three days after issuing its ultimatum, Beijing announced that the fortifications (probably fictional) had been dismantled. No more was said about the sheep and yaks, but shortly after the cease-fire was announced, citizens of New Delhi paraded 800 sheep past the Chinese Embassy. The sheep were covered with slogans saying: "We are here. No need to start a war!"

Turning Point: The War of 1971

During the war of 1965, the Pakistani Government had left East Pakistan only lightly defended, but the Indians had been too busy in western regions to take advantage of this fact. This neglect by the Pakistani Government, however, had not been missed by the people or politicians of East Pakistan. On the contrary they recognized it as part of a pattern of neglect, a pattern they had come to resent deeply.

The **Muslim** Bengalis who lived in East Pakistan formed 54 percent of the whole country's population, but Urdu, the language of the West Pakistani elite, had been chosen as the national language, rather than Bengali. West Pakistan had more doctors per person, as well as more colleges. It took 66 percent of U.S. aid, leaving only 34 percent for the more highly populated East. Only 5 percent of Army officers, and only 16 percent of high-ranking civil servants, were Bengalis from East Pakistan. Pakistan's new custom-built capital, Islamabad, was situated in West Pakistan.

This inequality upset many East Pakistanis. Their most popular political party, Sheikh Mujib's Awami League, developed a "Six Point Program" for fixing things. In essence the six points added up to the creation of separate **parliaments** in East and West Pakistan. These regional parliaments would deal with all domestic issues, including economic policy, leaving only foreign and defense policy to a national government.

As long as the Army remained in power in Pakistan, the Awami League had no hope of introducing this program. But the military defeat in 1965 cost the Army, and its leader Ayub Khan, a great deal of their previous popularity, and over the next five years opposition to the regime grew at a steady pace. In 1969 Ayub Khan was finally forced out, and his military successor, Yahya Khan, was pressured into promising elections in October of the following year. It was decided that the newly elected government would draw up a new **constitution** for the country.

From elections to civil war in Pakistan

At this stage few commentators expected an Awami League victory, but Yahya Khan took precautions just in case. In March 1970 he issued a "Legal Framework Order" that set limits on what a new government could do. It would not be allowed to tamper with Pakistan's "territorial **integrity**," by which he meant its current borders. If it did so, then Yahya Khan would have the right to dismiss that government. The main party in the West, Zulfiquar Bhutto's Pakistan People's Party (PPP), was happy to accept such restrictions. The Awami League, on the other hand, was not so happy, but it campaigned hard and successfully, winning 160 of the 162 seats in the East, and thus gained a majority in the 300-strong national assembly.

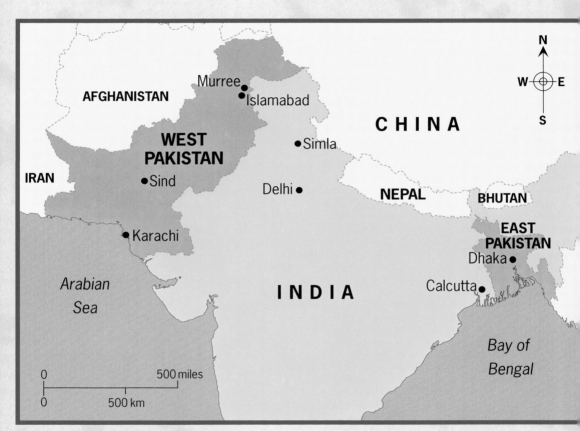

East and West Pakistan

The PPP, which had won 88 of 138 seats in the West, refused to accept the result. This provoked Sheikh Mujib into publicly announcing that Pakistan's new constitution would be based on the League's "Six Point Program." In March 1971 Yahya Khan held talks with Mujib in the Bengali capital Dhaka, but Mujib refused to budge. Convinced that the Awami League's ultimate aim was the East's **secession** from Pakistan, Yahya postponed the meeting of the new assembly. On the following day, the Awami League called a **general strike**, and East Pakistan ground to a halt. The protests started off peacefully, but were soon out of

Biography – Zulfiquar Ali Bhutto

Born in Larkana, Sind, Zulfiquar Ali Bhutto (1928–1979) studied in California and Oxford before becoming Pakistan's minister of commerce at the age of 30. He took over as foreign minister in 1963, and in 1965 he was a prominent voice demanding war with India and the capture of Kashmir. After Pakistan's defeat he founded the Pakistan People's Party (PPP), which quickly became the dominant party in West Pakistan, winning a large majority there in the 1970 election. His refusal to accept the Awami League's victory in East Pakistan (and Pakistan as a whole) doomed the country to the **civil war** of 1971, which ended with a second partition, and the creation of Bangladesh. At the Simla peace talks of 1972, he reportedly promised to abandon Pakistan's claims for Indian-occupied Kashmir, but claimed that he could not make this abandonment public and still remain in power.

Bhutto initially retained his popularity in the new, smaller Pakistan, which he led, first as president and then as prime minister, until 1977. However, the **world recession,** which began in 1973, seriously affected the economy, and a rising tide of protests eventually engulfed him. He was overthrown by a **military coup** in 1977, sentenced to death for conspiring to murder a political opponent, and executed in 1979. His daughter, Benazir Bhutto, eventually took over the leadership of the Pakistan People's Party, serving two terms as prime minister in the 1980s and 1990s.

Zulfiquar Ali Bhutto, surrounded by supporters in 1969.

control. If Sheikh Mujib had not been determined to secede before, he was now, and visits from Yahya Khan and Zulfiquar Ali Bhutto failed to change his mind. On March 25, 1971, the Pakistani Army, which was mostly composed of West Pakistanis, was sent in to restore order.

Most of the East Pakistanis in the Pakistani Army refused to fight against their own people, and eventually many of them took up arms on the side of a newly independent Bangladesh. For the moment, though, the Army could be as brutal as it thought necessary. Between March and December 1971, at least 300,000 civilians were killed. Ten million **refugees** fled across the frontier to India, Pakistan's traditional enemy.

India intervenes

In India, where Indira Gandhi had been prime minister since 1966, the country's leaders watched the Pakistan crisis develop with intense interest. If India helped the East Pakistanis against the West Pakistanis, then the new state of Bangladesh (which means "Bengal state") was likely to be friendly. This would improve India's strategic situation: it would no longer be sandwiched by the two wings of a hostile Pakistan. And there was also the growing problem of East Pakistani refugees crossing the border into India. India could not support so many hungry mouths indefinitely, and most would be unwilling to return home while the Pakistani Army remained in control.

India threw its weight behind the Bengali rebels, gently at first, but with increasing force as the year went on. Sheikh Mujib's Awami League was allowed to open an office in Calcutta, and to announce, on April 17, the establishment of a Bangladeshi **government-in-exile**. Pakistani planes were not allowed to use

Indian airspace, which tripled their flight time between West and East Pakistan. Most significantly of all, the Indian army started to train, arm, and provide bases for the Mukti Bahini, the main Bengali resistance group fighting for Bangladeshi independence. The Mukti Bahini eventually grew to more than 100,000 people.

After the Battle of Khulna, Indian troops stand guard over Pakistani prisoners.

Inside East Pakistan the **civil war** raged on through the summer and fall, becoming more and more ferocious. On November 22 the Mukti Bahini launched a major offensive, which was supported by Indian artillery across the border, and probably by Indian Army units deployed inside East Pakistan. Angry and exasperated Pakistanis struck back at India itself, trying on December 3rd to destroy the Indian Air Force on the ground with a series of coordinated surprise attacks. The attempt failed;

most of the Indian planes were protected in reinforced concrete bunkers, and the Pakistani attack missed those that were not. India's retaliation the next day was more successful. Many Pakistani Air Force planes were destroyed on the ground, and an air attack on Karachi destroyed important oil installations and effectively closed the harbor.

India and Pakistan were once more at war, but this was to be the shortest of their major contests. The Pakistani Army, worn down by nine months of civil war in the East and now deprived of most of its air cover, fell back before determined attacks. Indian forces occupied 5,000 square miles (13,000 square kilometers) of Sind in the West and surged toward Dhaka in the East, reaching its outskirts on December 6, 1971. Eleven days later the government in New Delhi again bowed to international pressure and declared a **unilateral cease-fire**. Three days after that, Yahya Khan resigned. Zulfiquar Ali Bhutto, who had been equally responsible for the war and subsequent defeat, took over as Pakistan's new leader.

Zulfiquar Ali Bhutto and Indira Gandhi sign the Simla Accord [Agreement], July 2, 1972.

Biography—Indira Gandhi

Daughter of Congress leader Jawaharlal Nehru, Indira Gandhi (1917–1984), no relation to the Independence campaigner Mahatma Gandhi, was born in Allahabad. After serving as president of Congress and minister of information in her father's government, she became prime minister in 1966. She tried, with some success, to reinforce India's **secular** traditions and reduce poverty, and her 1971 victory over Pakistan turned her into a national heroine. However, her policies were seriously undermined by the impact of the post-1973 **world recession,**

and her popularity dropped alarmingly. Found guilty of cheating in an election, she refused to accept the verdict, instead declaring a **state of emergency,** which lasted for two years, and which resulted in serious abuses of power. To her credit, when she submitted herself for reelection in 1977 and lost, she accepted her defeat.

Indira Gandhi in 1971, the year of her army's decisive victory over Pakistan.

When a substantial portion of the Congress Party rejected her leadership, she broke away to form the Congress (Indira) party, and led it to victory in the 1980 election. The next four years were marked by various threats to India's unity, most notably from the **Sikhs** in the Punjab. She took a hard line against them, and against those in Kashmir and elsewhere who wanted greater independence. In Kashmir her heavy-handedness backfired, increasing secessionist sentiment in the state and paving the way for an **insurgency**. She was assassinated by her Sikh bodyguards in 1984, and was succeeded as prime minister and leader of Congress (Indira) by her elder son Rajiv.

The Simla Accord

In two weeks the leaders of Pakistan had lost half of their country. Bangladesh was recognized as an independent state by most of the world's powers early in 1972. And there was still victorious India to deal with.

Talks at Murree and Simla in the summer of 1972 produced the Simla Accord between India and Pakistan. The Indians evacuated the area they had occupied in Sind, and returned all the 93,000 prisoners of war they had taken, including those whom Bangladesh had wanted to put on trial for **war crimes.** In exchange all Pakistan had to do was to repeat its promise not to use force to settle its disputes with India, and to "respect" the renamed **cease-fire** line in Kashmir—from this point on it would be called the Line of Control.

There were reports that Bhutto had privately agreed that the Line of Control should become, in time, more than a cease-fire line. It should, he said, become the permanent border between the two countries. For the moment, though, nothing was said in public. Both Bhutto and the Indians knew that such an agreement would cause enormous anger in Pakistan—the people would see it as defeat—and it would probably lead to Bhutto's downfall.

India had been generous, but it could afford to be so. Pakistan had been greatly weakened, and in one important way the situation in Kashmir had been transformed: with the emergence of Bangladesh, Pakistan's claim to represent all the **Muslims** of the subcontinent had been fatally undermined. India's stunning victory had made Indira Gandhi a national heroine, and most Indians now hoped and believed that they had finally put their problems with Pakistan and Kashmir behind them.

Promises, promises

"In Jammu and Kashmir, the line of control resulting from the cease-fire of December 17, 1971, shall be respected by both sides without prejudice to the recognized position of either side. Neither side shall seek to alter it unilaterally, irrespective of mutual differences and legal interpretations. Both sides further undertake to refrain from the threat of the use of force in violation of this line."
Article IV (3) of the agreement signed at Simla on July 2, 1972

Troubles at home

Pakistan

Discredited by their humiliating defeat, the Pakistani generals took a back seat and handed over leadership to the Pakistan People's Party (PPP). When a new **constitution** was adopted in April 1973, Bhutto became prime minister. He claimed that his policies were progressive and that they would produce a redistribution of wealth in favor of ordinary people, but little of this actually happened. When the **world recession** began in 1973 and the Pakistani economy stopped growing, the upper and middle classes clung to what they had. There was no extra wealth to share among the poor, and as the decade wore on, there were increasing signs of mass discontent.

Bhutto reacted by growing more **dictatorial,** imprisoning opponents, and increasing **censorship** of the media. Such actions only made matters worse, and there was growing support for those parties that favored a bigger role for **Islam** in the way the nation was run. Nine of these parties, whose increasing influence reflected the **Islamic revival** taking place throughout the **Muslim** world, came together as the Pakistan National Alliance to fight the January 1977 elections. They lost to the PPP, but Islamic protests continued, and for several months there was frequent rioting in the major cities of Pakistan. In July 1977 the Army, under General Zia ul-Haq, stepped in and overthrew Bhutto, imprisoning and then executing the former prime minister. New elections were promised, but repeatedly postponed. Military rule was reinstated in Pakistan.

The Army succeeded in imposing order for a while, but the country's basic problems—a huge gap between rich and poor, an oversized military machine, widespread **corruption,** and bitter **ethnic** feuds—did not go away.

In 1979 two immense upheavals—the Islamic revolution in Iran and the Soviet invasion of Afghanistan—shook the whole Muslim world. Both these events, and the enormous influx of Afghan **refugees** that followed the latter, gave strength and inspiration to Pakistan's Islamic **militants.** General Zia tried to silence Islamic opposition by introducing strict Islamic law in Pakistan, but as the 1980s unfolded, the country grew increasingly unruly and more prone to violence.

After Zia was killed in a plane crash in 1988, elections were held, bringing the PPP back to power, this time under the leadership of Bhutto's daughter, Benazir. For a short time, it seemed possible that Benazir Bhutto, the first female leader of a Muslim country, might be able to heal the country's divisions and mute the strident Islamic **nationalism** that was beginning to inflame both Kashmir and Pakistani relations with India. However, the divisions were too deep and the nationalist feelings too strong for her to overcome them.

General Muhammad Zia ul-Haq (speaking into the microphone) is sworn in as President of Pakistan, September 16, 1978.

India

Despite their victory in 1971, India and Indira Gandhi soon found themselves facing much the same problems as Pakistan and Zulfiquar Ali Bhutto. The world recession hit the Indian economy just as hard, driving the poor deeper into debt and threatening millions with starvation. Through late 1974 and early 1975, strikes and mass protests grew larger and more violent. Indira Gandhi was accused of incompetence and corruption, and in June 1975 she was found guilty of cheating in the previous election. Rather than accept a six-year ban from holding political office, she declared a national **state of emergency,** and ruled for the next two years as a virtual dictator. Many opposition politicians were jailed and strict **censorship** enforced. Indira Ghandi's younger son Sanjay became his mother's enforcer, running "slum clearance" and "forced sterilization" campaigns that rode roughshod over the rights of ordinary people and claimed many innocent lives.

Indira Gandhi declares India to be in a state of emergency, June 26, 1975.

Despite its many horrors, the **state of emergency** did produce some economic growth, and Indira Gandhi decided in 1977 that she could call and win an election. She lost but the new Janata Party Government lasted only two years. In 1980, her sins apparently forgotten, Indira Gandhi returned in triumph. Her joy was short-lived. Later that year Sanjay Ghandi was killed in an airplane accident, and her government soon found itself faced with mounting economic and political problems. The most serious of these was a **Sikh** rebellion in the Punjab. There was a long history of Sikh demands for greater **autonomy** within India, but now many Sikhs—most of whom lived in the Punjab—were intent on total independence. As the 1980s unfolded, violent protests and Sikh acts of **terrorism** became increasingly common.

Indira Gandhi let her police, security, and armed forces loose in the Punjab. The Sikhs' sacred Golden Temple in Amritsar was stormed; there were mass arrests and disappearances, illegal executions, and widespread intimidation. Those arrested were tortured to give up the names of others, who were themselves then tortured to give up more names.

This brutal oppression worked, at least in the short term, but it also cost Indira Gandhi her life. In October 1984 she was assassinated by her Sikh bodyguards. Her elder son Rajiv succeeded her as prime minister, but his initial popularity soon faded. Like Benazir Bhutto in Pakistan, he looked young and energetic enough to introduce real changes, but was unable to deliver. Following elections in 1989, the **Hindu** nationalist Bharatiya Janata Party (BJP) became the junior partners in a **coalition** government, and later that same year a Hindu **fundamentalist** march on Ayodhya wreaked untold damage on Hindu-**Muslim** relations. At a time when India needed it most, a tolerant, **secular** approach was nowhere to be seen.

Angry Sikhs demonstrate in New Delhi, 1984, after hearing that their Golden Temple in Amritsar had been occupied by Indian troops.

Ayodhya

According to **Hindu** legend, Ayodhya, in the Indian state of Uttar Pradesh, was the birthplace of the god Rama and the site of an ancient temple built to commemorate him. In the early 1500s the Mogul ruler Babur built a **Muslim** mosque on this sacred Hindu site, and by the end of the 1980s this had become one of India's most sacred Muslim **shrines**.

In 1990 Hindu fundamentalists organized a mass march to the site. Their plan—to destroy the mosque and rebuild the old temple—was actively encouraged by the BJP (then a junior partner in the government coalition), and enjoyed the support of most Hindus. The government, led by Prime Minister V.P. Singh, was determined to preserve India's reputation as a **secular** nation in which all religions were equally respected, and refused to allow the destruction of the mosque; police stopped the march in its tracks. The BJP withdrew its support from the government, which fell from power two weeks later.

The succeeding Rajiv Gandhi government was faced with the same problem two years later, but this time the mob managed to break through the police lines and demolish the mosque. Thousands of Muslims and **Sikhs** were killed by rejoicing Hindu fundamentalists in the widespread riots that followed.

Hindu fundamentalists scramble across fences and demolish the Ayodhya mosque, December 1992.

Kashmir

Victory in the 1971 war, and the Simla Accord of 1972, offered the Indian Government one last chance to create a political relationship with Kashmir that satisfied both itself and the Kashmiri population. They allowed the "Lion of Kashmir," Sheikh Abdullah, to resume power in Srinagar, and signed a deal with him —the Kashmir Accord of 1975—that seemed, in theory at least, to offer both sides most of what they wanted. Kashmir was given less real autonomy than earlier Indian promises had implied, but its special status was still recognized. In practice, as many Muslim Kashmiris soon pointed out, Kashmiris had been left free to do whatever they liked, provided that they did not annoy the Indian Government.

However, Sheikh Abdullah won the Kashmir state elections in 1977, and on the surface things seemed to be going well. The central government provided large amounts of money for rural electrification and educational improvements. The **literacy rate** went up by over 40 percent between 1973 and 1983. The tourist industry boomed, as increasing numbers of travelers flocked to the Vale, where they hired houseboats on Lake Dal and enjoyed the beauty of the surrounding snow-capped mountains. When Sheikh Abdullah died in 1982, he was succeeded by his son Farooq, who led the National Conference to victory in the state elections of 1983.

The BJP

The Bharatiya Janata Party, or BJP, came to prominence in the 1980s. It was the first major Indian political party to distance itself from the secular tradition created by the Congress Party, and to put Hindu interests above those of other communities. It wants India to be a Hindu state in the same way that Pakistan is a Muslim state. As such, it has little time for the wishes of Muslim Kashmiris, preferring the complete integration of Kashmir into India.

Beneath the surface, trouble was brewing. Many of the Muslim Kashmiris saw the Kashmir Accord as a betrayal, and there was a surge in the number and size of Islamic groups willing to challenge the National Conference Party. Increasing economic difficulties—in particular the lack of job opportunities for the growing number of graduates—further lowered the popularity of the Conference and boosted that of the Islamic groups.

The behavior of the Indian government made matters worse. Indira Gandhi was frightened that Kashmir might follow the **Sikhs** into outright rebellion, and she was angry with Farooq Abdullah of Kashmir's National Conference Party for refusing to fight the 1983 elections in partnership with her Congress Party. She spent much of 1984 plotting against him, and finally succeeded in securing his dismissal a few months before her own death. She had already appointed Shri Jagmohan as governor in Srinagar, and the new state government became little more than a mouthpiece for the central government in Delhi. A series of anti-**Muslim** measures produced a predictable increase in the number of violent protests and increasing support for the **Islamic** groups. The countdown to the **insurgency** had begun.

Supporters of the Hindu fundamentalist BJP Party at a rally to "Save Kashmir, Save India" in May 1990.

Renewed tension

Through the 1970s, with Kashmir quiet and many internal problems to deal with, India and Pakistan each focused on their own internal affairs. But in 1979, with the Islamic revolution in Iran and the Soviet invasion of Afghanistan, there was a dramatic increase in U.S. aid—both economic and military (weapons)—to Pakistan, which bordered Afghanistan. The Indians protested that such weapons might one day be used against them, but the United States did not change its policy.

Through the 1980s relations between India and Pakistan steadily deteriorated. In 1984 the two sides confronted each other on the Siachen Glacier in northern Kashmir. Having each staked a claim, both countries felt obligated to stay and defend it. During this same period, India claimed, probably with justification, that General Zia ul-Haq was giving hidden support to the Sikh rebels in the Punjab. In response the Indians arranged threatening military exercises close to the Pakistan border, which provoked fresh crises in both 1986 and 1987.

When Benazir Bhutto succeeded General Zia in 1988, it was hoped that she and Rajiv Gandhi—a new generation of leaders—might ease the strain between their two countries. However, they only reached an agreement not to attack each other's nuclear facilities. As the conflict between Muslim Kashmiris and the **Hindu**-dominated central Indian Government escalated, so their supporters in Pakistan and India were drawn once more toward conflict.

Paradise lost

"I was born in Kashmir. I grew up in its apple orchards and lush green meadows, dreamed on the banks of its freshwater streams. I went to school there, sitting on straw mats and memorizing tables by heart. After school my friends and I would rush halfway home, tear off our uniforms, and dive into the cold water. Then we would quickly dry our hair, so our parents would not find out what we had done.

"My village lies in the foothills of the Himalayas. During summer breaks, we would trek to the meadows high in the mountains, sit round a campfire and play the flute for hours. The chilling winter would turn the boys and girls of our small village into one huge family—huddled together in a big room, we would listen to stories until late in the night. Sipping hot cups of the traditional salt tea, the village elder, who had inherited the art of storytelling would transport us to the era of his tales. He had never been to school, but he remembered hundreds of beautiful stories by heart. Kashmir was like a big party, full of love and life. Today death and fear dominate everything."
Kashmiri journalist Muzamil Jaleel, who grew up in Kashmir during the 1960s and 1970s

Turning Point: the Kashmir Insurgency

Before the state elections of 1987, the Indian Prime Minister Rajiv Gandhi pressured Farooq Abdullah into agreeing that their two parties, the Congress Party and the National Conference Party, would fight the election as partners. The two-party partnership won, but there was a widespread feeling in Kashmir that the vote had been rigged. Many Kashmiri **Muslims** opposed to Indian rule began transferring their support from the Conference to one of the various Islamic groups.

Through 1988 and 1989, the situation in Kashmir steadily deteriorated. There were **intercommunal** riots in Jammu and Ladakh, and frequent **strikes** in the Vale. Farooq Abdullah's state government seemed powerless to impose order in Kashmir. **Militant** Islamic groups campaigned aggressively for support in all the towns of the Vale, including Srinagar. The most popular of these groups was the Jammu and Kashmir Liberation Front (JKLF), which supported complete independence for Kashmir. Other groups favored unification with Pakistan.

The beginning

"I was in Kashmir when the first bomb exploded in 1988. People first thought it was the outcome of a small political feud, although everybody knew the pot was boiling after years of political discontent. Then that September a young man, Ajaz Dar, died in a violent encounter with the police. Disgruntled by the farce of decades of [pretend] **democracy** *under Indian rule, a group of Kashmiri young men had decided to fight. They had dreams of an independent Kashmir. . . . Although this young man was not the first Kashmiri to die fighting for this cause, his death was the beginning of an era of tragedy."*
Muzamil Jaleel, writing in London's Observer **newspaper about the first bombing of the Kashmir Insurgency**

The Insurgency begins

The fuse that finally detonated the **Insurgency** was lit in December 1989, when the JKLF kidnapped Dr. Rubaiya Sayeed. She was the daughter of Mufti Muhammad Sayeed, a Kashmiri Muslim who served as a minister in India's central government. The kidnappers demanded the release of five imprisoned militants in return for Dr. Sayeed's release. The central government released the militants. While this sign of apparent weakness greatly encouraged the Islamic militant groups, the simultaneous reappointment of Shri Jagmohan as governor of the state (he had resigned the previous July) enraged most moderate Muslim Kashmiris. Farooq Abdullah promptly resigned as Kashmir's prime minister, saying that he could not work with "a man who hates the guts of Muslims."

An Indian soldier stands in front of a Kashmiri village destroyed during the Insurgency.

On the night of January 19, 1990, over 300 suspected Islamic militants were arrested in Srinagar. The next day a huge protest march of Muslim Kashmiris brought the city to a virtual halt. As the marchers approached the Gawakadal Bridge over the Jhelum River, Jagmohan's security forces opened fire. More than 100 people were killed, many of them shot, the others drowned as they sought escape in the icy waters of the fast-flowing river.

This massacre was barely mentioned in the Indian press, and those foreign correspondents who filed reports were quickly expelled from the Vale. Curfews were introduced in Srinagar and other towns. Kashmiri calls for an inquiry were ignored. This incident started a new phase. It was no longer a fight between the militants and the security forces. It was now a total **insurgency,** or rebellion, of the entire population.

V.P. Singh flashes a victory sign at his supporters during the Indian general election of 1989.

The central Indian government dissolved the state government and reinforced the local police with paramilitary and military units; by the end of February 1990, an extra 100,000 men had been deployed in Kashmir. But demonstrations continued to fill the streets. Over 400,000 Kashmiris surrounded the offices of the

UN Military Observer Group in Srinagar to demand the implementation of old UN resolutions, and in early March more than 40 demonstrators were killed when the security forces again opened fire on an unarmed crowd.

What Amnesty International said

"The brutality of torture in Jammu and Kashmir defies belief. It has left people mutilated and disabled for life. The severity of torture meted out by the Indian security forces in Jammu and Kashmir is the main reason for the appalling number of deaths in custody."
From Amnesty International's January 1995 report, "Torture and Deaths in Custody in Jammu and Kashmir." *Amnesty International investigates and reports on the treatment of political prisoners throughout the world.*

International impact

The insurgency came at a particularly bad time for the V.P. Singh and Benazir Bhutto governments, which at that time were trying to improve their relations with each other. Benazir Bhutto, in particular, found it impossible to ignore the swelling chorus of support in Pakistan for the Kashmiri rebels. She condemned the violent Indian response to the demonstrations, and made increasingly outspoken calls for a free Kashmir, by which she meant union with Pakistan. Either with or without her agreement, the Pakistani military began moving its troops around in a deliberately threatening manner. The V.P. Singh government in Delhi, which depended for its majority on the support of the **Hindu** nationalist BJP, started moving its own troops toward the Pakistani border. V.P. Singh called on Indians to be "psychologically prepared" for a war with Pakistan.

Tensions reached a peak in April 1990, but talks between the two foreign ministers in New York produced a temporary easing of the situation. In early May relations took another turn for the worse, and an all-out war involving the use of nuclear weapons began to look possible. Warnings from the United States defused the situation. In New Delhi the United States told the Indians to behave with more restraint in Kashmir. In Islamabad the United States pointed out that every India and Pakistan confrontation had ended in a Pakistani defeat.

The Indian army, seeking out militants thought to be hiding, round up Kashmiri men and check their identification, August 1995.

The insurgency continues

In Kashmir itself, and particularly in the Vale, the fighting showed no sign of letting up throughout 1990 and 1991. In May 1990 the funeral of a **Muslim** leader was attacked by Indian security forces, who claimed that they themselves had been attacked. A hundred mourners were shot dead, and even the coffin was peppered with bullets. In the outcry that followed, Kashmir Governor Shri Jagmohan was dismissed, but the central government continued its policy of fighting with every method at its disposal, both legal and illegal. According to **human rights** organizations, thousands of suspects were imprisoned without trial, tortured, killed in custody, or they simply "disappeared." Villages or towns accused of sheltering militants were searched, looted, and frequently burned. Many Muslim women were raped by members of the security forces, in what some critics believed was part of a deliberate attempt to intimidate the whole population.

Thousands of innocent young Kashmiri Muslims were arrested on suspicion of being involved with the opposition. Many others, thinking they were likely to be arrested, chose to join one of the armed resistance groups, which were busily establishing bases in the mountains on both sides of the **cease-fire** Line of Control. These groups ambushed Indian patrols and mounted attacks on isolated Indian posts. They also began receiving increasing assistance—money, recruits, and weapons—from outside Kashmir. Pakistani governments played a part in this, but more help was provided by those Islamic organizations that had spent the last decade fighting the Soviets in Afghanistan, and that were now based in both Afghanistan and Pakistan. For these men Kashmir had become another holy war.

An unhappy peace

Despite this increased outside involvement, the Indian Government managed, through sheer force of numbers, to bring the rebellion under some sort of control by the mid-1990s. This was achieved in part by turning the Line of Control into a heavily fortified border, complete with listening devices, motion detectors, and antipersonnel mines. By 1995 as many as 400,000 Indian soldiers, police, and other security forces were stationed in Kashmir, almost one for every twenty of the Kashmiri population. The Indian Government also tried, somewhat belatedly, to win over former Kashmiri moderates with concessions—new elections, the freeing of some prisoners, and promises of more in the future. This slightly softer approach persuaded few. As one Kashmiri put it, "How could we ever accept the Indian government again, after what the military did to our people?"

The militants were also facing problems. As the government campaign against them grew more effective, the supply of recruits and funds dried up, and the militants' new policy of "asking" Kashmiri families for either money or "a son for the struggle" caused increasing resentment. There were also splits developing within the militant camp, between native Kashmiris and outsiders, between those who wanted independence and those who preferred union with Pakistan, between those who supported continuing the war and those who favored a return to peaceful protest.

Nuclear Weapons

India's nuclear program began in the 1950s, under the leadership of Prime Minister Nehru. At this stage India had no intention of creating nuclear weapons, but merely wished to master nuclear technology and use it to generate electricity. However, a series of alarming events—the defeat by China in 1962, the explosion of a Chinese nuclear device in 1964, and the threatening appearance of a nuclear-armed U.S. aircraft carrier during the 1971 war with Pakistan—persuaded India's leaders to develop their own nuclear weapons. In May 1974 a device was successfully tested in the Rajasthan desert.

This picture of the site of an Indian nuclear test in the 1970s was not released until 1998.

The Pakistanis, stung by their defeat in 1971, had also begun their own nuclear program. Since they had no history of peaceful nuclear development to build on, it took them longer to gather the necessary knowledge and materials. No tests were conducted, but by the early 1990s it was widely assumed that Pakistan had some sort of nuclear capability. The United States certainly thought so. In 1993 the **Central Intelligence Agency** warned of the dangers of a nuclear war between India and Pakistan, and one study by an influential U.S. organization estimated that such a war would kill 2 million people instantly, and another 100 million in the weeks, months, and years following the war.

In 1998 the guessing game was finally brought to an end. In mid-May India tested a series of five nuclear devices, and two weeks later Pakistan followed suit. In both countries the tests were conducted for political, rather than scientific reasons—both governments were eager to persuade their own people how strong they were. In both India and Pakistan the tests met with wild approval from the general population, and even wilder threats from politicians to wipe the other country off the map.

It is unclear if the knowledge that both countries have nuclear weapons makes war more or less likely. Some experts argue that neither country will dare to launch a nuclear attack, because both know that the other will retaliate with a nuclear attack of its own. Other experts disagree. They point out that missiles fired by either country have very little distance to travel, which makes a surprise attack on the other country's missiles possible. Since neither can afford to be caught by such an attack with their missiles on the ground, the temptation to strike first might become irresistible in a time of crisis.

Love and hate

In India the nation's atomic bomb is called the *swadeshi* or home-grown bomb, as if it represented a fulfillment of Mahatma Gandhi's longing for Indian self-sufficiency. Gandhi was a peace lover, however, and would most likely have been opposed to Indian ownership of nuclear weapons. Although many people in India and Pakistan would prefer peace to conflict, popular support for nuclear weapons remains strong in both countries.

Turning Point: Kargil Conflict of 1999

There have been violent incidents between Indian and Pakistani (or Pakistani-backed) troops along the Line of Control in Kashmir since it was first established as a **cease-fire** line in 1949. But some time periods and areas have seen more activity than others. During late 1997 and early 1998, there were several outbreaks of fighting in the mostly empty far-northern Kargil area, as each side tried to intimidate the other. At first the rest of the world chose to ignore these violent gestures, but the nuclear tests of May 1998 changed all that. Suddenly the conflict around Kargil was the possible trigger for a nuclear war. The United States applied pressure to both India and Pakistan to improve their relations.

Nawaz Sharif meets U.S. President Clinton in Washington, July 1999.

Atal Bihari Vajpayee on the new cross-border bus, February 1999.

In response the Indian Prime Minister Atal Bihari Vajpayee, whose **Hindu** nationalist BJP party had won the election of 1998, and the Pakistani Prime Minister Muhammad Nawaz Sharif, held several rounds of friendlier-than-usual talks. In February 1999, in an effort to symbolize peaceful cooperation between the two countries, Vajpayee personally opened a new bus service across the border between India and Pakistan. He also took the well-intentioned step of visiting the site in Lahore where Jinnah had first suggested the creation of Pakistan more than 50 years earlier. It seemed as though relations between the two countries were improving faster than anyone had dared to hope.

A patrol is lost

This was an illusion. Pakistan's political and military leadership was deeply unhappy about the situation in Kashmir, and had decided to do something about it. As they saw it, the insurgency was quickly running out of steam, India was reimposing its authority, and the chances of a settlement in Pakistan's favor were disappearing. Taking advantage of the apparently improved relations between the two nations, the Pakistani leadership set about devising and implementing a plan to get the insurgency going again.

On May 5, 1999, an Indian patrol in the Kargil area moved into the high mountains. Its orders were to find out whether the snow on the upper slopes had melted enough for the army to reoccupy those positions it had left during the harsh winter months. The patrol was never seen or heard from again. More were sent out to look. Air reconnaissance was stepped up. Over the next week the Indians discovered that roughly 100 intruders had dug themselves in at high altitude on the Indian side of the Line of Control. Over the week that followed, the figure was revised upward to 800. The intruders were spread out at intervals along a 93-mile (150-kilometer) front, and were equipped with artillery, snowmobiles, and enough supplies to last them several months. There had been a mini-invasion of Indian-controlled Kashmir.

Forcing these intruders back across the Line of Control was easier to order than to achieve. The Pakistanis and their allies from **Muslim**-controlled Azad Kashmir had taken the highest and best positions, and their Indian attackers, forced to advance across open slopes, suffered serious casualties. The Indian government decided to use its air force against the intruders, the first time it had been used in Kashmir since 1971. More than 550 flights were flown, and many of the intruders were killed or wounded by bombs, but they were not driven out. The Indians returned to their original plan, and began the costly process of recapturing the occupied positions with ground troops.

To the brink

The Pakistanis and their Azad Kashmiri allies hoped that by prolonging this process they could force the rest of the world to pressure India over Kashmir. However, as the Indians slowly captured one outpost after another, it became increasingly apparent that this was not going to happen. At some point in late May or early June 1999, it seemed likely that the decision was taken in Islamabad to raise the stakes even higher. Both sides put their nuclear forces on the highest alert and began preparing their missiles for firing.

Indian forces use mobile rocket launchers against Islamic insurgents in Kashmir, July 1999.

This was the most serious nuclear crisis since the Cuban Missile Crisis of 1962, and it was only resolved by enormous U.S. pressure on Pakistan. Nawaz Sharif was called to Washington and told that all U.S. aid to Pakistan would be suspended if the intruders were not withdrawn. The fighting went on for several more weeks, but slowly, reluctantly, Pakistan pulled its men back across the Line of Control.

Pakistan's leadership had lost its miniwar, and any reputation it had for being trustworthy. As the Indians were quick to point out, the plot to infiltrate the Kargil area must have already been underway while Nawaz Sharif was still entertaining Vajpayee in Lahore. How could India ever trust Pakistan again?

It was not all bad news from Pakistan's point of view. Kashmir was in the headlines once again, and impossible for the rest of the world to ignore. The **insurgency** had indeed been reactivated, at least for a while. Through the summer of 1999, **militant** activity increased, with frequent attacks on army posts and camps. The tourist trade dried up once more, with devastating effects on the local economy. In September the general election was mostly boycotted by Kashmiris, and the Indian Government retaliated by arresting many of the leading **Muslim** Kashmiri politicians. A lasting peace between India and Pakistan, and the Kashmiri settlement that would make such a peace possible, seemed as far away as ever.

Leaders since partition

India

1947–1964	Jawaharlal Nehru (Congress)
1964–1966	Lal Bahadur Shastri (Congress)
1966–1977	Indira Gandhi (Congress)
1977–1979	Morarji Desai (Janata)
1979–1980	Charan Singh (Lok Dal)
1980–1984	Indira Gandhi (Congress [I])
1984–1989	Rajiv Gandhi (Congress [I])
1989–1990	V.P. Singh (Janata Dal/BJP)
1990–1991	Chandra Shekhar (Janata Dal)
1991–1996	Narasimha Rao (Congress [I])
1996	Atal Bihari Vajpayee (BJP)
1996–1997	Deve Gowda (United Front)
1997–1998	Inder Kumar Gujral (United Front)
1998–	Atal Bihari Vajpayee (BJP)

Pakistan

1947–1948	Muhammad Ali Jinnah (Muslim League)
1948–1951	Liaquat Ali Khan (Muslim League)
1951–1953	Khawaja Nazimuddin (Muslim League)
1953–1955	Mohammad Ali Bogra (Muslim League)
1955–1956	Chaudhri Mohammad Ali (Muslim League)
1956–1957	Hussein Shaheed Suhrawardy (Awami League)
1957	Ismail Chundrigar (Muslim League)
1957–1958	Malik Feroz Khan Noon (Muslim League)
1958–1969	Ayub Khan (military rule)
1969–1971	Yahya Khan (military rule)
1971–1977	Zulfiquar Ali Bhutto (PPP)
1977–1988	Zia ul-Haq (military rule)
1988–1990	Benazir Bhutto (PPP)
1990–1993	Mian Muhammad Nawaz Sharif (Muslim League)
1993–1996	Benazir Bhutto (PPP)
1996–1997	Malik Meraj Khalid (PPP)
1997–1999	Mian Muhammad Nawaz Sharif (Muslim League)
1999–	Pervez Musharraf (military rule)

India and Pakistan in the Media

Over the last 50 years the conflict between India and Pakistan has filled acres of newsprint and hours of broadcasting time, both in the two countries themselves and in the world at large. The wars have been reported shot by shot, the dispute in Kashmir analyzed from every possible angle, and the reasons for the two countries' hostility endlessly discussed. But are the reports accurate and unbiased?

The wider world

During British rule many inhabitants of the subcontinent, both **Hindu** and **Muslim,** were allowed or encouraged to live and work elsewhere in the British Empire, in places like South Africa and the West Indies. Most such migrants and their descendants still feel an emotional attachment to the subcontinent. They are able to stay informed about developments there by reading locally produced newspapers in their own language. Films are another way of keeping in touch with cultural roots—the successful Bombay-based film industry is often known as "Bollywood." Since independence many more people have migrated to the developed world, particularly to the United States and Great Britain.

Indian shops line this street in Iselin, New Jersey. Many cities in the United States have large Indian and Pakistani communities.

Indians scan their daily papers for news of their country's relations with Pakistan.

Broadcasting

The governments of India and Pakistan inherited government control of radio and television broadcasting from the British. Over the years both have used their control of these media to promote a sense of national unity, rather than to encourage the spread of accurate and unbiased reporting. In India, particularly over the last two decades, serialized epic presentations of Hindu legends have celebrated Hindu values and offered a definition of national pride that often seems to exclude non-Hindus. In Pakistan, state television and radio have given an ever greater emphasis to the promotion of **Islam** as the bond that holds their nation together.

Newspapers

The newspapers in both countries have traditionally been privately owned, and, particularly in India, are often highly critical of the government in power. When it comes to reporting the conflict with their neighbors, however, the press in both countries has not always presented a balanced view. During actual wars, governments in most countries impose **censorship,** and this has been the case in each of the India-Pakistan conflicts.

India also made life extremely difficult for reporters in Kashmir during the **insurgency,** restricting their access to places and people in order to cover up the many breaches of **human rights** committed by its security forces.

Indian and Pakistani journalists, however, have shown a tendency to accept such restrictions on their freedom of access and expression. Where disputes between the two countries are concerned, they often act as little more than mouthpieces for their respective governments. As in other conflicts around the world, so during the Kargil War both newspapers and TV were full of stories of brave soldiers at the front and extended coverage of funerals, both designed to increase patriotic feeling. There were few, if any, attempts to question the human and economic costs of the conflict, or to present the other side's point of view.

Bowler Wasim Akram of Pakistan "dismisses" India's Rahul Dravid in the Cricket World Cup, 1999.

Such biased reporting extends beyond the news media. For example, the reporting of cricket matches between the two countries is often used as a way of expressing their mutual hostility. In 1999, during the Cricket World Cup in England, the *India Express* declared that a match between the two nations was "the next best thing to war." Similar sentiments were expressed in the Pakistani press. In India at this time, a computer game called "I love India" was on sale. One aim of the game was to destroy the Pakistani city of Lahore.

How the world sees India and Pakistan

Increasing numbers of Indians and Pakistanis have access to global media, and in particular to international news channels and magazines, especially those originating in the United States and Britain. U.S. coverage of South Asia, both for international and American audiences, tends to be sparse. There are few historical connections between the two regions. British coverage is more thorough, reflecting the large numbers of British citizens with Indian and Pakistani roots, but the area is still relatively neglected.

The actual coverage is restricted in several ways. News programs traditionally concentrate on new and dramatic events and downplay continuing processes. This means eruptions of violence in Kashmir receive more attention than attempts to rebuild trust in communities badly affected by the insurgency. The possible impact on British and U.S. viewers also helps determine what gets read or shown. A nuclear war between India and Pakistan would affect them, but a few soldiers throwing artillery shells at each other on a glacier miles from anywhere does not.

Finally, the British and U.S. press bring their own prejudices to the reporting of the conflict between India and Pakistan. As the representatives of **secular** democracies, the journalists of both countries have tended to identify more with secular India, although the recent growth of **Hindu fundamentalism** has undermined this connection. Pakistan, on the other hand, has been adversely affected by Western fears of **Islam** becoming stronger—fears that increase with each major crisis in relations between the West and the Islamic world, like the Gulf War of 1991, the September 11 terrorist attacks on the United States, or the Iraq war of 2003.

Turning Point: September 11

After the Kargil War of 1999, Pakistan's international situation deteriorated sharply. Waging an aggressive war in Kashmir, and threatening the whole region with a nuclear holocaust, had antagonized even the country's friends. The United States, upon whom Pakistan traditionally relied for economic and military assistance, was particularly angry, and the **military coup** that overthrew the **democratically** elected Nawaz Sharif government in October of the same year angered the United States still further. The fact that it was led by General Pervez Musharraf, the man widely believed to have been the architect of the Kargil operation, only made matters worse. Rarely in Pakistan's 55 years of independence had the country's reputation sunk so low.

In the spring of 2000, the situation in Kashmir flared up again, and Pakistan agreed, under intense pressure from the United States, to hold more talks with India. Musharraf and Indian Prime Minister Vajpayee met in July, and the atmosphere at first seemed surprisingly friendly. But the basic differences between the two sides—India's insistence that Kashmir was only in turmoil because of Pakistani interference; Pakistan's insistence that the whole province was still a matter of dispute between the two countries—soon soured proceedings. In the end the two sides could not even find enough common ground to issue a joint statement. They agreed to have more talks at some indefinite future date, but few saw any hope of breaking the deadlock.

September 11 and the War on Terrorism

This was the situation on September 11, 2001, when members of the Islamic terrorist organization al-Qaeda hijacked four U.S. airliners and successfully crashed three of them into the World Trade Center in New York City and the Pentagon in Washington, D.C. It is thought that the fourth plane, which crashed in rural Pennsylvania, was targeting the White House. The U.S. Government, with substantial international support, declared a war on terrorism in general, and on al-Qaeda in particular.

The leadership of al-Qaeda was based in Afghanistan, where it enjoyed the protection of that country's Islamic **fundamentalist** rulers, the Taliban. Pakistan shared a land border with Afghanistan, and any U.S. planes using aircraft carriers in the Indian Ocean would need to fly over Pakistani territory to reach Afghanistan. The Pakistani government and intelligence services also had close contacts with the Taliban, whom they had helped install as the rulers of Afghanistan. Suddenly, the United States needed Pakistan.

Stunned onlookers watch smoke pour from the stricken World Trade Center, September 11, 2001.

This was good news for the Musharraf government, in that it ended Pakistan's period of isolation. It was also worrying news, because many Pakistanis supported the aims, if not always the methods, of both the Taliban and al-Qaeda. If Musharraf supported the United States too much, he risked being overthrown by his own people. If he didn't support them enough, there was a good chance he would be added to the

Biography—Pervez Musharraf

Born in New Delhi, Pervez Musharraf (1943–) and his family moved to newly independent Pakistan after several years in Turkey. Musharraf joined the Pakistan Army in 1964, and served in the wars of 1965 and 1971, winning a medal for bravery in the first. In later years he commanded both armored divisions and infantry brigades, achieving the rank of general in 1998. He was widely believed to have planned the Pakistani incursion into Kashmir, which triggered the Kargil War of 1999, and later that year he led the bloodless **military coup** that overthrew the elected government of Nawaz Sharif. He appointed himself the nation's "chief executive," upgrading his title in 2001 to president. He promised to restore democracy by holding elections in 2002, but then imposed conditions. Only college graduates could stand, and the PPP leader Benazir Bhutto (herself a graduate) was specifically prohibited from taking part.

Pakistani leader Pervez Musharraf, speaking to Kashmiri refugees on February 5, 2000.

list of enemies that the United States intended to confront. It could be argued, and frequently was by India, that Pakistan was itself supporting **terrorists** in Kashmir.

This turn of events was also mixed news for India. The United States made every effort to reassure India that it would not favor Pakistan at India's expense, but in Delhi any plus for Pakistan was considered a minus for India. On the other hand, the new emphasis on defeating terrorism gave India the perfect excuse to point out that Pakistan was in league with all sorts of **Islamic** terrorists, from the groups it supported in Kashmir to those it had helped in Afghanistan.

There was soon fresh evidence of terrorism in Kashmir. Less than three weeks after the attacks in the United States, Islamic **militants** attacked the Kashmiri **parliament** in Srinagar, leaving 38 dead. India protested that Pakistan was to blame, and called on the United States to share their condemnation. The United States, fearful of losing Musharraf as an ally with the war in Afghanistan not yet underway, refused to condemn such actions publicly. Instead, the United States lectured the Pakistani leader in private on the need for an end to his country's active support for the Kashmiri militants.

The war scare of 2002

On December 13, 2001, two months after the outrage in Srinagar, terrorists struck in New Delhi itself, killing twelve people in an atttack on the Indian Parliament. India blamed the attack on Pakistani-backed Islamic groups and the Pakistani intelligence organization, the ISI. Pakistan denied any connection to the attackers. Both sides began moving large numbers of troops toward their mutual frontier, and on January 11, 2002, India's Chief of Staff announced that his country was "ready for war." He also said that India would not hesitate to use its nuclear weapons if Pakistan used them first.

As 2002 unfolded the tension grew, and by May a large-scale war between the two countries seemed to be a real possibility. International pressure and self-restraint on the part of the two governments prevented that, but there was no return to normal peacetime conditions. Hundreds of thousands of soldiers continued to line the frontier, and there was artillery shelling across the Line of Control in Kashmir almost daily. The two sides made regular accusations of unprovoked attacks by the other, as they have consistently done in every such situation since 1947.

Prospects

The partition is more than 50 years old. Several major wars and countless violent incidents later, the armed forces of India and Pakistan are still at odds. Kashmir is still a source of resentment and violence.

What can be done about Kashmir? There are two basic options. The first would be to let the people of Kashmir decide, as was the intention all those years ago. Separate **plebiscites** could be held in all the main areas, giving the different populations a three-way choice between union with Pakistan, union with India, or independence. It seems likely that such a vote would result in Ladakh and Jammu sticking with India, and the Northern Territories and perhaps Azad Kashmir sticking with Pakistan. How the vote in the Vale would go is unclear.

Indian police on patrol in Kashmir during the local elections of September 2002.

The problem with this option is that India is unlikely ever to accept it. Giving up Indian Kashmir, or even a part of it, would be seen as a strategic loss, an economic loss, a blow to Indian pride, a betrayal of India's **secular** foundations, and an invitation to other regions of India to seek their own independence. Meeting the wishes of the Kashmiris might be an admirable ambition, but not if it led to the breakup of India.

The second option involves an acceptance of the current Line of Control as the permanent border between the two countries. This would not be welcomed by many Vale Kashmiris, but time and a measure of real **autonomy** from Delhi might lead most to accept it. In the past India has both offered and withdrawn this solution. Pakistan has always refused it. Only enormous outside pressure could force a change of heart in either country, and only the United States has the power to exert such pressure. The situation would require pressure on Pakistan to accept the border, and pressure on India to provide Kashmiris with increased autonomy, because without the latter, Pakistan would be unable to escape the accusation that it had betrayed its fellow **Muslims.**

Even this option, however, is unlikely to be implemented in the foreseeable future. The United States, though worried by the possibility of a nuclear war in South Asia, is currently preoccupied by the War on **Terrorism.** In India even Kashmiri autonomy is seen by many as a threat to the stability of the whole union. In Pakistan, itself increasingly threatened by internal divisions, the national dream of recapturing Kashmir represents a desperately needed unifying force. To give up that dream for Indian promises of good behavior in the Vale would be almost unthinkable.

So it is likely there will be more misery for Kashmiris, more murders, bombings, and police repression. Along the Line of Control there will be more ambushes, more shelling, and more deaths. There will probably be more major wars. There will certainly be more money spent on high-tech weapons than these two countries can afford. The situation is not hopeless— there are people on both sides who know only too well that the continuing conflict serves no useful purpose—but the immediate prospects are not good.

Appendix

Chronology of events

1947 *August* Independence for India and Pakistan

October Maharajah of Kashmir officially agrees to join India

1947 India and Pakistani forces clash in Kashmir

1948 *January* India refers Kashmir question to UN Security Council

1948–1949 Series of UN resolutions on Kashmir

1949 *January* Establishment of cease-fire line in Kashmir

1953 Indian government removes Sheikh Abdullah as prime minister of Kashmir

1954 Pakistan joins Western alliance SEATO

1962 *September–November* India's war with China

1963 Extensive but fruitless talks on Kashmir between India and Pakistan

December Sacred relic stolen from mosque in Kashmir

1964 Death of Jawaharlal Nehru

1965 *January–April* Armed conflict in Rann of Kutch sparks second India-Pakistan war

August–September Armed conflict in Kashmir spreads to Punjab and Sind

1966 Tashkent summit; Indira Gandhi becomes prime minister of India

1970 Elections in Pakistan won by secessionist Awami League

1971 *March* Civil war breaks out in East Pakistan

November India intervenes in East Pakistan, sparking third India-Pakistan war

December Birth of Bangladesh

1972 India and Pakistan sign Simla Accord

1974 India detonates first nuclear device

1975 Kashmir Accord agreed on by Indira Gandhi and Sheikh Abdullah

1975–1977 State of emergency in India; Indira Gandhi loses election

1977 Zulfiquar Ali Bhutto government in Pakistan overthrown by Army, ushering in eleven years of military rule under General Zia ul-Haq

1979 Iranian revolution and Soviet invasion of Afghanistan help create a global upsurge of Islamic fundamentalism

1980 Indira Gandhi returns to power

1981 Sikh insurgency begins in India's Punjab

1982 Death of Sheikh Abdullah

1983 Farooq Abdullah wins Kashmir elections

1984 Fighting breaks out on Siachen Glacier in northern Kashmir

June Indira Gandhi engineers dismissal of Farooq Abdullah

October Indira Gandhi assassinated by Sikh bodyguards

1986–1987 Military exercises cause tension on India-Pakistan border

1987 Elections in Kashmir rigged by India

1988 General Zia ul-Haq killed in plane crash; Benazir Bhutto becomes Pakistan's prime minister

1989 *October* First march on Ayodhya

December Kashmir Insurgency begins

1990 *April–May* More tension on India-Pakistan border

1990 Heavy government repression in Kashmir

1992 *December* Destruction of mosque at Ayodhya

1993–1995 Nature of Kashmir insurgency changes, from largely homegrown rebellion to war directed by Islamic groups originating outside Kashmir

1998 *March* First Hindu nationalist majority government elected in India

May India, and then Pakistan, conduct nuclear tests

1999 *April–June* Fighting in Kargil region leads to nuclear alert

October Nawaz Sharif government in Pakistan overthrown by General Musharraf

2000 *July* Unsuccessful talks about Kashmir between Indian and Pakistani governments

2001 *September* Terrorist attack on New York City and Pentagon

December Terrorist attack on Indian parliament in New Delhi

2002 *May* Mobilization of Indian and Pakistani armies on border leads to fears of war

Further reading

Crompton, Samuel Willard. *Pakistan.* Broomall, Penn.: Chelsea House, 2002.

Cumming, David. *The Changing Face of India.* Chicago: Raintree, 2002.

Dalal, Anita. *Nations of the World: India.* Chicago: Raintree, 2001.

Goodwin, William. *Pakistan.* Farmington Hills, Mich: Gale Group, 2002.

Wagner, Heather Lehr. *India and Pakistan.* Broomall, Penn.: Chelsea House, 2002.

Useful websites

http://www.cnn.com/WORLD
CNN news

www.amnesty.org
Amnesty International

Glossary

accession act of joining

autonomy self-rule, often for a particular area or community within a larger state

Buddhist follower of Buddhism, a world religion based on the teachings of Buddha

cease-fire declaration of an end to a period of fighting

censorship limiting of free expression in newspapers, books, films, etc.

Central Intelligence Agency (CIA) U.S. federal bureau responsible for intelligence and counter-intelligence activities outside the United States

civil war war between different groups within one country

clique small, exclusive set of people

coalition temporary alliance, often of political parties or nations with a common goal

constitution in politics, the statement of the way a country is set up to safeguard its fundamental principles

corruption immoral practices such as bribery and fraud

democracy political system in which government is conducted either by the people directly or by their elected representatives

democratic relating to a democracy of or for all people

dictatorial acting as a ruler with total power

ethnic relating to groups in society with distinctive cultural traits

feudal ancient system of land ownership

fundamentalism relating to belief in the literal truth of a sacred text

general strike refusal of workers in all industries to work, as a means of protesting unfair practices or policies

government-in-exile when a government is forced to flee the country and tries to set up from another country

Hindu believer in the main religion and social system of India, which traditionally features multiple gods, a belief in reincarnation (rebirth of a soul in a new body), and the caste system

human rights basic rights that should belong to any person

insurgency rebellion against a government

integrity completeness

intercommunal between communities, usually used to refer to two religious communities

irregulars soldiers not belonging to an official army

Islam one of the world's three major monotheistic (one God) religions (along with Christianity and Judaism), founded by the Prophet Muhammad in the 7th century

Islamic revival in recent history, the rise in the popularity of Islam as a solution to political problems that took place during the final quarter of the 20th century

literacy rate percentage of people in the population who can read and write

militant person who favors violent or confrontational action in support of a cause

military coup seizure of power by a country's armed forces

Muslim follower of Islam

nationalism feeling that people in a country or area all belong together and are different from people in other places. Also used to describe a belief in the superiority of your own country or ethnicity.

parliament lawmaking assembly that has usually been at least partly elected

plebiscite referendum or direct vote of the whole electorate, usually to answer a single important political question

refugee one who flees to another country for safety

secession act of breaking away from a larger state

secular not specifically religious, especially in reference to a government that keeps religion separate from other affairs of the state

shrine sacred place

Sikh believer in Sikhism, a monotheistic (one God) religion founded in the Punjab in the 15th century that contains elements of both Hinduism and Islam

state of emergency time when many rights (such as free speech) are withdrawn because a government has fears of violence

terrorism use of violence to achieve political ends

theater [of war] area that is or may become involved directly in war operations

unilateral one-sided

United Nations (UN) international body set up in 1945 to promote peace and cooperation between states

UN resolution judgment issued by the UN requesting or demanding particular action from parties involved in a dispute

veto to prevent something from happening by voting against it

war crimes crimes committed during wartime that are against the rules of war, such as killing civilians

world recession general slowdown of global economic activity

Index